MUSHROOMS

Nature's
FRIENDS

by Joyce Markovics

NORWOOD HOUSE PRESS

NORWOOD HOUSE 🏠 PRESS

For more information about Norwood House Press, please visit our website at: www.norwoodhousepress.com or call 866-565-2900.

Book Designer: Ed Morgan
Editorial and Production: Bowerbird Books

Photo Credits: Krysztof Niewolny/Unsplash.com, cover; Ruston Jones/Unsplash.com, title page; © iStock.com/Big Joe, 4; © iStock.com/Mirrorimage-NL, 5; Wikimedia Commons, 6; Wikimedia Commons, 7; freepik.com, 8; Jimi Malmberg/Unsplash.com, 9; © iStock.com/ttsz, 10; © iStock.com/Kichigin, 11; Justin Jensen/flickr, 12; © iStock.com/AnnekeDeBlok, 13 top; Wikimedia Commons, 13 bottom; freepik.com, 14; freepik.com, 15; Amee Fairbank-Brown/Unsplash.com, 16; freepik.com, 17; Wikimedia Commons, 18; © iStock.com/SHAWSHANK61, 19; Naja Bertolt Jensen/Unsplash.com, 20; mycobond/flickr, 21; © Bolt Threads, 22; © Photo by Kris Graves, courtesy of The Living, 23; Wikimedia Commons, 24; © iStock.com/Moha El-Jaw, 25; © Ed Morgan/navybluedesign.com, 27; freepik.com, 29.

Library of Congress Cataloging-in-Publication Data

Names: Markovics, Joyce L., author.
Title: Mushrooms / by Joyce Markovics.
Description: Chicago : Norwood House Press, [2023] | Series: Nature's
   friends | Includes bibliographical references and index. | Audience:
   Grades 2-3
Identifiers: LCCN 2021061186 (print) | LCCN 2021061187 (ebook) | ISBN
   9781684507658 (hardcover) | ISBN 9781684047789 (paperback) | ISBN
   9781684047840 (ebook)
Subjects: LCSH: Mushrooms--Juvenile literature. |
   Mushrooms--Ecology--Juvenile literature.
Classification: LCC QK617 .M396 2023 (print) | LCC QK617 (ebook) | DDC
   579.6/163--dc23/eng/20220106
LC record available at https://lccn.loc.gov/2021061186
LC ebook record available at https://lccn.loc.gov/2021061187

353N—082022

Manufactured in the United States of America in North Mankato, Minnesota.

CONTENTS

GIANT FUNGUS

In 1992, scientist Jim Anderson discovered a monster in a Michigan forest. It covers an area as big as 180 football fields. It weighs about as much as three blue whales. On top of that, it's more than 2,500 years old! This **ancient** living thing is not a monster. It's a single fungus.

A fungus is a living thing that can't make its own food. (*Fungus* is the singular form of the word. *Fungi* is the plural form.) Visitors named the organism that Jim found the "**humongous** fungus." "It caused quite a stir," said Jim when he first identified it. Nobody believed that one fungus could be that big or old.

Armillaria gallica is the scientific name for the fungus. These are the fungus's mushrooms.

The forest in Michigan where Jim Anderson located the giant fungus

People travel from all over the world to visit Michigan's humongous fungus.

Jim returned to the forest in 2015 and 2017. He tested samples of the humongous fungus, including its mushrooms. Jim proved that it was, in fact, one very old **organism**. The words *fungi* and *mushrooms* are often used to talk about the same thing. Yet they're two different things.

The umbrella-shaped, honey-colored mushrooms of *Armillaria gallica*

Mushrooms are only a small part of fungi. They help fungi **reproduce** much like an apple on an apple tree. The rest of the fungus is made up of mycelium (mahy-SEE-lee-uhm). The word *mycelia* is the plural form of *mycelium*. This large web of tiny, twisting threadlike parts grows underground.

Mycelium make up the main body of a fungus.

NEVER TOUCH OR EAT A MUSHROOM YOU FIND OUTSIDE. IT MIGHT BE POISONOUS!

FUNGI FACTS

Fungi have lived on this planet for a long time—around forty million years. They grow all over the world, even in icy Antarctica. Fungi come in all shapes and sizes, although most are very small. Scientists believe there are four million kinds of fungi. That's ten times more fungi than plants on Earth! Fungi also includes molds, mildews, and yeasts. Only about 20,000 fungi are known to produce mushrooms.

Different kinds of mold growing in a petri dish

Fungi are not animals or plants. They look a little like plants. However, they can't use the Sun's energy to make food. They grow out in all directions to find food. Then they break it down using their rootlike mycelium. Fungi make **chemicals** that **dissolve** food outside their bodies. Then they absorb the **nutrients**.

Some fungi are very colorful like this poisonous fly agaric mushroom.

9

The mycelium's thread-like parts are called hyphae (HAHY-fee). The hyphae take in nutrients. They also get rid of waste. However, the mycelium is much more than a network of roots. Fungi use their mycelia to communicate!

For example, if a certain fungus is under attack, it can send signals through its mycelia. The signals might tell the fungus to release bad-tasting chemicals. The chemicals may stop a hungry animal from eating the fungus.

This diagram shows mushrooms and mycelia.

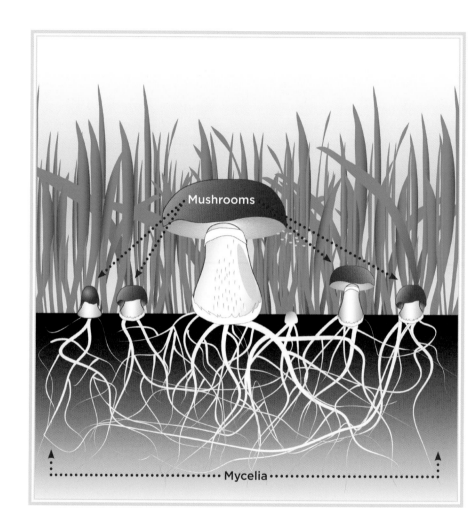

Mushrooms

Mycelia

A mycelium can grow to cover a huge area. Unlike mushrooms that often live for a few days, mycelia can live for thousands of years. This explains Jim's 2,500-year-old humongous fungus!

This photo shows both mycelia and hyphae. They look a little like cobwebs.

Just one teaspoon of soil can contain more than 6 miles (9.7 km) of hyphae!

Fungi use mushrooms and spores to reproduce, or make new fungi. Spores are tiny cells. Inside each spore is everything needed to form a new fungus. Spores are often found under the domed cap of a mushroom. Many mushrooms have plates called gills that hold spores. Though not every mushroom stores spores like this. Some, such as cup fungi, hold their spores in cuplike parts. Puffballs are mushrooms that look like spongy spheres. They hold spores inside their round bodies.

Cup fungi in Costa Rica

Depending on the type, mushrooms release their spores differently. Millions of spores shoot out of gilled mushrooms onto the ground. Puffballs release their trillions of spores in a smoke-like cloud. Not long after, new mycelia start to grow from the spores.

A close-up view of puffball spores

These puffball mushrooms are releasing a cloud of spores.

Spores come in a huge variety of sizes and shapes. Some are starlike or branched. Others look like coiled snakes.

RECYCLERS

Fungi are nature's **recyclers**. They often grow in forests or fields. Here, they break down plant matter, such as leaves and old trees. Some fungi **decompose** dead animals as well. Fungi turn dead things into nutrients. In the process, they release important chemicals, such as nitrogen, back into the soil. Thus, fungi help nutrients cycle through the **environment**.

These mushrooms are growing on a dead tree.

Fungi are also great partners to plants. As decomposers, fungi get rid of dead things. By doing this, they make room for new trees and other plants to grow. Some fungi also help feed plants. Their mycelia grow on plant roots, making it easier for plants to absorb nutrients. Mycelia can also deliver water to plants. In fact, some fungi have helped whole forests survive a **drought**!

Experts say that ninety percent of plants have a partnership with fungi.

Some kinds of fungi can rot solid wood and kill plants. They are known as parasites.

FOOD FOR ALL

Lots of animals love to eat fungi, especially mushrooms. Why? They're both **nutritious** and delicious. Deer often munch on mushrooms, even the poisonous kinds. Rabbits and squirrels are mushroom eaters also. Both snack on fungi, such as truffles, that grow underground. People prize truffles for their earthy flavor. Pigs and boars have great noses and can sniff out truffles in the soil. For this reason, people use trained pigs to find truffles!

A squirrel eating a mushroom

People enjoy eating a mix of mushrooms. Oyster, shiitake, and straw are popular varieties. They are fried, baked, and boiled. Not only are mushrooms tasty, they're also healthy! Mushrooms are packed with **vitamins** and **protein**. Studies suggest they help fight heart disease, cancer, and **diabetes**, too.

An assortment of mushrooms people commonly cook with

A leafcutter ant carrying a leaf piece

Insects dine on mushrooms also. Certain ants are fungus farmers! Leafcutter ants use their sharp jaws to snip off pieces of leaves. Then they carry the leaf bits back to their nest. Surprisingly, the ants don't eat the leaves. Instead, they use them to grow fungi.

The fungi grow on the chopped-up leaves. Over time, sweet round growths sprout from the fungi. The leafcutter ants pick these and eat them. When the leafcutter group moves to a new home, the ants carry spores in their mouths. Then they can grow a new fungus garden!

Leafcutter ants and their queen in their fungus garden

A group of leafcutter ants is led by a queen. She's much larger than the other ants.

MANY USES

In addition to being food for ants, fungi has other incredible uses. A fungus found in a landfill in Pakistan can break down plastic! It often takes many years for plastics to break down. However, this special fungus can decompose one type of plastic in a few short weeks. Fungi can tackle other kinds of pollution as well. Some fungi have the amazing ability to get rid of **toxic** waste, including **radioactive** materials!

Only about nine percent of all plastic waste is recycled. The rest ends up in dumps or the ocean.

What's also amazing is people are using fungi to replace plastic and Styrofoam. They've come up with a way to make packaging from mycelium threads. Hyphae can act like nature's glue to bind together wood chips, for example. This forms a strong material that's a lot like plastic or Styrofoam. Yet it's much better for the environment.

Packaging made from mycelium

How much plastic pollution is there? There's more plastic on Earth than 500 times the number of stars in the galaxy.

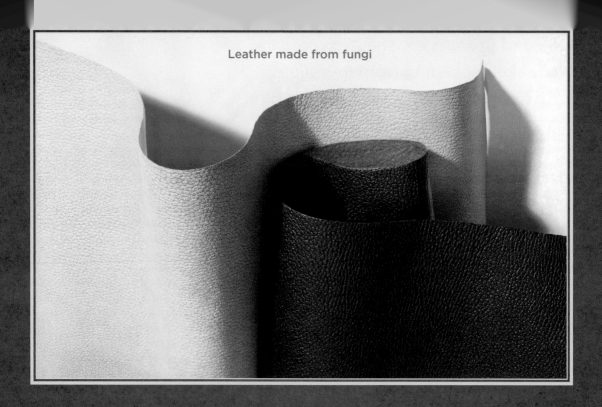

Leather made from fungi

In a similar process, people are making "leather" from fungi. This new leather-like material is used to create shoes, clothing, and more. That's not all. Scientists are exploring ways to make building materials from fungi. One scientist has developed a brick using mycelium and crushed glass.

"The possibilities for what we might use mycelium for are endless," says Gitartha Kalita, a scientist in India. He and other scientists use fungi and hay to make a material similar to wood. Fungi can grow on just about anything, even trash. "They can take our waste and turn it into something which is really valuable," Gitartha says. Using fungi in this way can help people live more **sustainably**.

This building was constructed using mycelium bricks.

23

MUSHROOM MEDICINE

Beyond useful products, fungi can also save lives! Around fifteen percent of drugs used by people come from fungi. One of the most well-known is penicillin. It's a kind of mold that kills bacteria. Bacteria causes some diseases and **infections** that can make people very sick.

Penicillium mold growing on an orange

Fungi are also used to make drugs called statins and steroids. Both treat illnesses that can be life-threatening. Certain mushrooms may also help with mental health problems. These problems include **depression** and anxiety. Experts are still researching how mushrooms affect people's health. However, they believe there's a lot to learn about how fungi can help people.

Mushrooms used for medicine

Experts are looking into ways mushrooms can be used to fight cancer.

A WORLD WITHOUT MUSHROOMS

What if there were no mushrooms? For one thing, there would be many more dead trees. Nutrients would not flow through the environment as efficiently. The plants that depend on fungi could die. Plus, the many animals that eat mushrooms would have less food. People would also not have access to products made from fungi. Lastly, there would be no more mushroom medicine.

For mushrooms to thrive, we can protect the places where they live. Leave dead trees alone, and don't pick mushrooms. Fallen trees are homes and food for many kinds of fungi. You can also be a mushroom **ambassador**! Tell others how fantastic fungi are.

These ink cap mushrooms look like tiny umbrellas.

IDENTIFY MUSHROOMS!

Mushrooms are more common than you think. There are two main places where mushrooms grow: fields and forests. Search these areas for different mushrooms, then draw, research, and identify them!

- Get a notebook and colored pencils.
- On a warm day, ask an adult to look for mushrooms with you outside. WARNING: NEVER TOUCH OR EAT A MUSHROOM YOU FIND OUTSIDE.
- Once you spot a mushroom, draw it in your notebook. Try to make your drawing as detailed as possible.
- Find two other mushrooms and draw them.
- At home, research the three mushrooms you found. Try to identify them by name.

AGARIC

MILK

PARASOL

HAPPY MUSHROOM HUNTING!

GLOSSARY

ambassador (am-BAS-uh-der): a messenger or representative.

ancient (AYN-shunt): very old.

chemicals (KEM-uh-kuhlz): natural or human-made substances.

decompose (dee-kuhm-POHZ): to rot or break down into another form.

depression (di-PRESH-uhn): a mental condition that makes people feel sad, inadequate, and tired.

diabetes (dye-uh-BEE-teez): a disease in which people have too much sugar in their blood.

dissolve (dih-ZAWLV): to break down substances in a liquid into smaller parts.

drought (DROUT): a long period of time with little or no rain.

environment (en-VYE-ruhn-muhnt): the area where things live and everything, such as weather, that affects that place.

humongous (hyoo-MUHNG-uhss): huge.

infections (in-FEK-shuhnz): illnesses caused by germs entering the body.

nutrients (NOO-tree-uhnts): substances needed by living things to grow and stay healthy.

nutritious (noo-TRISH-uhs): healthful and nourishing.

organism (OR-guh-niz-uhm): a living thing.

parasites (PA-ruh-sites): living creatures that get food by living on or in another plant or animal.

protein (PROH-teen): a kind of substance that keeps the body healthy and strong.

radioactive (ray-dee-oh-AK-tiv): giving off dangerous, invisible rays of energy.

recyclers (ree-SYE-klerz): living things that adapt other things for reuse.

reproduce (ree-pruh-DOOS): to have young.

sustainably (suh-STEY-nuh-blee): in a way that allows for continual use of a natural resource.

toxic (TOK-sik): poisonous or deadly.

vitamins (VYE-tuh-minz): substances in food that are necessary for good health.

FOR MORE INFORMATION

Books

Boddy, Lynne. *Humongous Fungus*. New York, NY: DK, 2021.
Readers will learn fascinating facts about fungi.

Gravel, Elise. *The Mushroom Fan Club*. Montreal, Quebec: Drawn and Quarterly, 2018.
Hunt for mushrooms in this fun, informative book.

Scott, Katie, and Ester Gaya. *Fungarium*. Somerville, MA: Big Picture Press, 2021.
This book explores an extraordinary collection of fungi.

Websites

Australia National Herbarium
(https://www.anbg.gov.au/fungi/what-is-fungus.html)
Read about fungus and mycelium.

Chicago Botanic Garden
(https://www.chicagobotanic.org/conservation/fungi)
Find out how to protect fungus.

National Park Service: So Many Mushrooms!
(https://www.nps.gov/articles/so-many-mushrooms.htm)
Readers can learn about more unusual mushrooms.

INDEX

ABOUT THE AUTHOR

Joyce Markovics has written hundreds of books for kids. She thinks fungi are fabulous. Joyce lives in an old, creaky house along the Hudson River. She hopes the readers of this book will take action—in small and big ways—to protect nature, one of our greatest gifts. Joyce dedicates this book to Natalia, a fellow mushroom lover, artist, and friend.